WINNING WITH

ACCOUNTABILITY

THE SECRET LANGUAGE
OF HIGH-PERFORMING ORGANIZATIONS

HENRY J. EVANS

WINNING WITH
ACCOUNTABILITY

THE SECRET LANGUAGE
OF HIGH-PERFORMING ORGANIZATIONS

Printed in the United States of America
ISBN: 978-0-9819242-0-5

Credits

Editor	Alice Adams, Austin, TX
Copy Editor	Kathleen Green, Positively Proofed, Plano, TX info@PositivelyProofed.com
Design, art direction, and production	Melissa Monogue, Back Porch Creative, Plano, TX info@BackPorchCreative.com

TABLE OF CONTENTS

Introduction   5

Chapter 1 - What Is Accountability, Really?   9

Chapter 2 - You Looking at Me?   21

Chapter 3 - The Language of Accountability   31

Chapter 4 - I Can See Clearly Now   45

Chapter 5 - It's Time to Get Specific   55

Chapter 6 - Ownership   65

Chapter 7 - Going Public   73

Chapter 8 - Your Role in Creating a   83
High-Accountability Culture

NEXT STEPS ...   89

INTRODUCTION

Those who act receive the prizes.
Aristotle

Successful teams cannot exist without accountability – high performance and accountability go hand-in-hand.

Accountability starts with understanding the truth and continues with the thoughts, words and actions of everyone involved in your organization. It is the key to long-term, sustained organizational success.

Execution fails when accountability – the process and language of transferring strategies into reality – is missing. If you have ever experienced a failure in a relationship or project, you may have found that, in hindsight, clear outcomes may not have been properly communicated to all of the players. If you could "do it all over again," there are things you would have said differently in order to enroll people on the front end of the effort.

Without accountability, people are working on the wrong things and feeling like they lack direction and purpose. When accountability is present, people keep their eyes on a very clear prize. They know what they are working toward and how they are going to get there. Accountability gives people and organizations a sense of purpose.

High-performing teams create success after they have infused accountability into their interactions and agreements.

This means that they have established their desired outcome and support the endeavor through the *thoughts, words* and *actions* of everyone involved in their organization.

This book will provide you and your organization a roadmap on how to win with accountability. It is based on how organizations have taken our accountability model and achieved success far beyond their expectations. The principles they applied are universal and will work in your organization as well.

Accountability is the secret language within your organization that can create or prevent success.

A few years ago, our firm Dynamic Results was contacted to help a large organization. This client's sales had been flat for more than two decades. They had attempted several "programs of the year," which added a little spark but no sustained flame to their results. They were desperate by the time we received their call.

This organization was built upon a sales network of independent dealers around the world. As you can imagine, communication and accountability were their greatest challenge.

After several fact-finding meetings, we introduced them to our simple, effective method for creating high-accountability cultures. Turning mediocrity into success in this organization – or any organization – is not instant or easy. After all, creating an accountability culture is a change. However, less than 24 months after implementing our accountability method, their sales doubled. In addition, job satisfaction, productivity and profits all improved dramatically.

The primary reason that this organization's results were flat was because accountability was missing in their strategy. There was not an agreed-upon, specific set of outcomes that everyone was diligently working toward. The "strategy" was the same ol' sales and grow-dealer-network mantra.

Our initial change was to map a strategy with specific, measurable outcomes. Then the client created timelines for making things happen instead of deadlines. The organization also changed its compensation and recognition programs to be in line with the specific results they were now focused on. And, for the first time, the client published their vision and strategy throughout the entire organization.

In just under two years after implementing the accountability method outlined in this book, the organization doubled its sales!

We are not claiming that our method caused this change by itself. In fact, the client did all the heavy lifting. The president of this company did, however, choose to acknowledge our team at their international conference, shining a spotlight on our team's table (the client had flown us all in) and said that they "would never have achieved the last two years' performance without the contribution by the team at Dynamic Results."

Winning with Accountability will take you step-by-step through the methods and tools they used to help achieve their objectives, which you can use to achieve yours, too.

In the first part of this book, we will define accountability, examine the leader's role in creating a high-accountability culture, and introduce the importance of language in creating successful outcomes.

Then, you will discover a proven process – The Four Pieces of the Accountability Puzzle – for successfully creating a culture of accountability in your organization.

Lastly, we will show you what actions you can take to begin creating a Culture of Accountability today. Relationships and projects fail when accountability is missing. Following the principles outlined in this book will help you lead your organization to higher performance and stronger relationships.

Read, learn, grow and begin *Winning with Accountability*.

> A Culture of Accountability makes
> a good organization great and
> a great organization unstoppable.

WHAT IS ACCOUNTABILITY, REALLY?

Hypocrisy exists in the space between language and action.

Picture yourself in a meeting. Suppose there are a dozen people seated around a table and someone says, "I'm going to hold you accountable for what we've discussed." What words or feelings immediately come to mind?

Fear? Threat? You may be thinking, "Uh oh, now there are expectations." Others around the table may experience pressure or stress. Still others sense the tone of the meeting suddenly has changed – leadership is going to be searching for a "gotcha."

This type of negative reaction to accountability has been earned. Most of us have experienced the word "accountability" as punitive – a "punishment" for not doing something. It is viewed as punishment because that accountability typically lurks at the back end of the business process. Accountability shows up when something goes wrong and people start to lay blame. They start pointing fingers.

In reality, winning begins with accountability. You cannot sustain success without accountability. It is an absolute requirement!

The secret that successful organizations have discovered is to install accountability on the front end of interactions ... before the outcome is known. Successful organizations front-load accountability into their strategy. When front-loaded, accountability breeds better relationships, eliminates surprises, and vastly improves job satisfaction and performance.

Defining Accountability

Accountability should not be defined as a punitive response to something going wrong.

Webster's Dictionary defines "accountability" as "the quality or state of being accountable; an obligation or willingness to accept responsibility for one's actions."

Notice the adjectives describing accountability in the dictionary: quality, obligation, willingness and responsibility. Does that sound like punitive response to something that has gone wrong? Of course not. Accountability means preventing something from going wrong.

So, as a first step on the road to creating an accountability culture, we must redefine and streamline "accountability" to carry a more positive connotation:

Accountability: "Clear commitments that — in the eyes of others — have been kept."

With this new definition in mind, let's put it to work by asking you to write down in the space below two commitments that are important to your success. One for business and one for your personal life.

Business Commitment _____

_____

_____

Personal Commitment _____

_____

_____

Thank you. We'll refer to these later in the book.

People deal with us based on what they think about us, not what we think they should think about us. So, when we make a commitment, we have to fulfill that commitment in the eyes of others. It is not good enough to fulfill the commitment in our eyes – we have to fulfill the commitment in the eyes of others. That is the tricky part.

When we're accountable, it is necessary for us to go to our customers, our suppliers, the people we work for – and yes, the people who work with us – and ask them, "How am I doing?" We allow them to hold us accountable – in their eyes – for our commitments.

Growing up in New York City during Mayor Ed Koch's administration, I remember this: Whenever Koch greeted someone, he'd say, "Hey, I'm Mayor Ed Koch. How am I doing?" He constantly asked for feedback. He was being accountable in his constituents' eyes.

Was Ed Koch the best mayor in New York's history? That depends on whom you talk to, but he continually asked for feedback ... and the voters loved it!

Accountability is – first and foremost – about being reliable. To get a good picture of your personal accountability, you may want to periodically ask yourself, "Can people count on me to do what I say I'll do, as I said I would do it?"

Recently, at a meeting involving the president, chairman of the board and chief operating officer of a large organization, an executive named Cathy promised, "You'll have the executive summary from this meeting by Friday, December 21, at 5 p.m. CST."

Two of the officers wrote down this information. The president did not; and when one of his colleagues asked him, "Aren't you going to hold Cathy accountable?" the president responded, "I've worked with Cathy for three years. I know she's as good as her word."

It's at that moment Cathy knew she had consistently acted in an accountable way. It was the president's perception and feedback that let her know she had modeled accountability.

Creating an accountability culture is to recognize that wherever you are on the organizational chart, you encourage others to hold you accountable.

For instance, let's say I'm sitting in my office working on a presentation. I asked my assistant to hold all calls and not disturb me while I focus on the presentation for an important meeting.

I hear the mailman leave my mail and, out of the corner of my eye, I see a new issue of a martial arts magazine. I love martial arts so I go over, pick the magazine up and begin leafing through it ... and, as usual, I find an article I'd like to read.

I return to my office and begin reading the article. It's at this point my assistant steps in and says, "Shouldn't you be working on the presentation that you asked me to allow you the time to focus on?"

I slowly close the magazine and smile. "Yes, thank you."

Now, saying "thank you" may not be the first thing that comes to mind at that moment, but my focus is on communicating genuine thanks. She's holding me accountable to my stated commitments because that's the deal we have, and I do appreciate her holding me accountable to getting the important things done.

Accountability is about high performance and not fear or stress. It's about being willing to hold yourself to a standard that improves the performance of your organization and also having a willingness to be held accountable by others.

So, it's okay that a member of your team walks into your office and says, "Hey, you said you'd have that report on competitive products to me by noon today. It's 1 p.m. When can I expect it?"

In an organization where accountability isn't important, the manager might say, "Wait a minute. Let's get this straight. You work for me. I don't work for you! Now, get out of my office!" But, in a Culture of Accountability, the manager will say, "You know what? I'm sorry I didn't get that to you on time. Here's when I'll have it for you."

When holding someone else accountable we must recognize and respect the power of intention. If our intention is to put someone down or to make them feel badly about themselves, it will be obvious. If, however, our intention is to help them perform at a higher level and to help them succeed, they will be able to see that, too.

Here's an example:

> While facilitating a meeting with a client, we were reviewing our performance with them and listening to their feedback. At one point during this discussion, I called a 10-minute break. At the moment the break began, one of my team members walked up to me with her back to the clients, a smile on her face, and very direct eye contact. She said, "Henry, you are being defensive and you have 9 minutes to adjust, okay?"
>
> A couple of hours later when the meeting had ended, we asked the president of the company for feedback on the meeting. He said, "You know, Henry, when the meeting started, I felt that you were being a little defensive, but right after I noticed it, it seems to have vanished. The meeting was a huge success."

I am eternally grateful to my team member for giving me the feedback when she did. I remember trusting her intention in that moment.

> "When you're screwing up and nobody says anything to you anymore, that means they've given up on you."
> **Randy Pausch**, author, *The Last Lecture*

Remember: *Hypocrisy exists in the space between language and action.*

If you are ever perceived as a hypocrite, it's because there is a gap between what you said and what you did. Hypocrisy is created in the space between your words and your actions.

This simple example explains the concept well: Erik is a new manager and he's having a team meeting. Chris has joined the group late because of a long meeting with an important client. He quietly asks the person next to him where they are on the agenda.

Erik's saying, "Employee morale is really important to me." Then he sees Chris asking about the agenda and shouts, "Be quiet, Chris!"

In a very short space, a lot of relationship damage has just occurred.

On the other hand, if Erik's been the team leader for awhile and if he's told his team, "If you ever interrupt one of my meetings, I'm going to tell you to be quiet" – and then he does exactly that – Erik's not a hypocrite because he's set a clear expectation.

How to Front-load Accountability

To front-load accountability in your organization, you have to provide the specifics … and that includes clear expectations. If your team can reflect the essence of what you said to them back to you, your expectations have been clearly stated. If their reflection does not mirror what you are trying to accomplish, you need to start again.

For instance, if I wanted Sam to reflect back to me, I wouldn't ask Sam to repeat what I said because that would be condescending. What I could say is, "Sam, how do you interpret what I just said?"

Another way to invite reflection is by asking someone to paraphrase what they heard you say.

Front-loading accountability begins with clear expectations from both the sender and the receiver. And, it is both parties' responsibility.

For instance, what if your manager told you, "I expect you to do a good job on this proposal."

You could say, "Okay" and take your best shot at meeting the manager's expectations. Or, you could say, "Okay, but exactly what does a good job look like?"

The manager may say, "I want our products to be featured up front, which should be followed by features and benefits. Then, in the summary, show how our products resolve the client's accounting problem."

In this example, the manager provided the details and how the assignment would be measured. By providing the measurements for the project – at the beginning of the project – the manager has allowed you to succeed in doing a good job.

If you are not provided the specifics of what a good job looks like, you probably won't succeed, which makes it important to ask the question, "What does a good job look like?" or "What does it mean when you say, 'Good job'?"

So, what if you make an assignment and you're not completely clear on what the outcome may be? If that is the case, consider this language:

"I'm not 100 percent sure the decision we're making is going to be the right one. However, everybody needs to be 100 percent sure this is the decision we've made and this is the direction we're going to take. We may have to adjust later."

To use this language successfully takes trust. It takes honesty for the leader to say, "I don't have a crystal ball ... and I accept that I may be wrong. But everyone needs to understand that this is our direction and this is how we're doing it."

The next step to front-loading accountability is to put into place a high testing standard to measure quality. Just as important, you must be willing to take feedback and make changes that will strengthen your strategy. Part of this feedback will come from team members, and more feedback will come when you ask your customers, "How am I doing?" In doing so, you're getting feedback from every level throughout the process.

The Benefits of Front-loading Accountability

Remember when we asked you to think about how being asked to be accountable made you feel? Quite often people have feelings of stress, fear or being extremely uncomfortable.

The term "accountability" probably deserves these negative connotations when it is used in a punitive way ... and in Western cultures, we tend to use accountability to determine whom to punish when something has gone wrong.

These feelings of fear, stress and discomfort when we are asked to be accountable are what we call "relationship breakers." So, when accountability comes at the backend of the business process, we break that very thing that pulls us through tough times and fuels good times: relationships.

Conversely, **when you front-load accountability, relationships will be built, solidified and strengthened**.

When you front-load accountability, you include specificity in your commitment. Unlike the manager who asked team members to "do a good job" on the important client proposal, your commitments include specific language – "I want this proposal to outline our products at the beginning, include features and benefits and, in the summary, to show how our products will resolve their current accounting problem. Here is when I need it to be completed."

Front-loading accountability is also a hiring function. Many winning organizations make accountability a part of their hiring process, specifically addressing personal accountability in interviews. Those organizations make it policy to only recruit and retain employees who embrace accountability as part of their personal values.

In describing accountability to one new employee, the hiring manager said this: "Accountability in our organization means doing what you said you will do, as you said you would do it. That is the minimum acceptable performance level for our team members. It's the way we are ... and it's a high standard."

When you front-load accountability:

- ✦ Performance increases

- ✦ Resources are better allocated – people don't have to guess

- ✦ Job satisfaction is increased

- ✦ Relationships are strengthened

- ✦ Results improve, ultimately increasing revenues and profitability

Summary:

✦ Accountability is a positive term describing commitments that – in the eyes of others – have been kept.

✦ Accountability is continually asking, "How am I doing?"

✦ To front-load accountability in your organization, you have to provide crystal-clear expectations.

✦ By front-loading accountability, relationships among team members are strengthened because they know they can count on each other. This leads to greater performance, higher quality and better service to your clients.

You Looking at Me?

The higher you are on the org chart, the fewer people there are who are willing to hold you accountable.

Creating a Culture of Accountability requires time, patience and vision. Creating that culture begins with you … and you will find you have a tremendous amount of influence, wherever you are on the organizational chart.

The late Mahatma Gandhi provides an illustration of how others are influenced by someone consistently modeling the behavior they want to change.

Gandhi was an unknown man with a big vision – India's independence from the British Empire, the world's greatest superpower during the early 20th century. Living simply, Gandhi made his own clothes (a simple shawl and a loin cloth) and underwent long fasts for reasons of both self-purification and protest. While Gandhi was not the originator of the principle of nonviolence, he was the first to apply it on a national scale. He replaced armed resistance across India with civil disobedience and nonviolent demonstrations.

"Be the change you wish to see in the world," Gandhi counseled. Often, against great odds, he modeled his vision to create the change he was destined to achieve.

In 1945, after almost 30 years of peaceful resistance and non-cooperation, India won its independence from Great Britain.

One of the greatest challenges in creating a Culture of Accountability is to be like Gandhi – consistently modeling the changes that need to be made to achieve your vision. Yes, everyone in your organization is constantly watching you and the behavior you are modeling. You are always leading!

For instance, let's suppose that you are conducting a meeting to introduce a new business strategy. Periodically, Kristin – one of your brightest employees – interrupts you in mid-sentence. You soon notice a pattern of Kristin's interruptions in meetings and it is driving you crazy.

How do you react? Are you complaining to others about Kristin? Probably not the best idea. Do you call Kristin into your office and chastise her for interrupting you in meetings? Also not a good solution.

Instead, a better choice may be to model the change you want to see in Kristin. You make sure you never interrupt Kristin in a meeting … or anywhere else, for that matter. The behavior you model will, at least, create the possibility of Kristin behaving differently in meetings. You do not criticize her with what you want to see in meetings. You show her the behavior you want her to reflect.

Like Gandhi, you can "be the change you wish to see in the world." In other words, "go first!"

Another example would be if someone is consistently late to your meetings, be on time for theirs.

Go first!

If someone is withholding information that would make you successful, provide them with the information that will help lead to their success.

Go first!

Whatever your role in your organization, you are highly visible to many people. They are watching your every move, interpreting the meaning behind it, and sharing their interpretations with others.

Even with the status that comes with leadership positions, there are drawbacks. The higher you are on the organizational chart, you probably have fewer people who will step forward to hold you accountable and tell you if you're aligning your thoughts, words and actions with your desired outcomes.

Remember the Wizard in *The Wizard of Oz*? He was the little guy who hid behind a green velvet curtain while he pushed all the buttons and created the wizard-like sound effects. If you think you're fooling people when you feel one way and say something else, you're like that little wizard … except you're hiding behind a curtain that is transparent … like a clear-plastic shower curtain.

Everybody inside and outside of the organization can see how you really feel, how you act and whether what you say is aligned with what you do. **You are accountable for the influence you have on the organization's culture – no matter what position you hold on the organizational chart.** That's why it's important to look at ourselves first and the contributions we make to the culture when we see something that's not working for the benefit of the organization.

After many years consulting with major corporations, my theory is that if managers look first at themselves when searching for the origin of a problem, the organization moves forward at an accelerated rate. In fact, the more people in an organization who are looking at themselves, the greater the impact on the organization.

If you look for someone to blame for your problems, you may be relieved to put the blame elsewhere, even though it actually delays solving the problem. However, anytime you put the cause of your problem in someone else's hands, you are – knowingly or unknowingly – surrendering your power and, simultaneously, your own influence.

The Theory of Looking First at Ourselves

So, what's your role as you build a high-accountability culture?

Socrates, the Greek philosopher, wrote: "Let him that would move the world first move himself."

Leo Tolstoy, the Russian novelist and philosopher, said: "Everyone thinks of changing the world, but no one thinks of changing himself."

The common thread? They're saying, "First, focus on yourself."

The Mirror/Glass Concept

If you've ever seen a television *Law and Order* series, you have no doubt seen suspects taken into an interrogation room. In that room, there is at least one mirrored wall ... or so it appears to the suspect.

But, what's on the other side of that mirrored window or wall?

If you said, "a glass window where detectives and others can see and hear everything the suspect says without being seen," you're right!

It's the same in the police lineup room. The victim can sit behind a one-way glass and identify the perpetrator without the "perp" being able to see them ... because, inside the lineup room, the one-way glass looks like a mirror.

In his terrific book *Good to Great,* Jim Collins introduced the concept of leadership mirror and glass. Here's how the mirror-glass concept works for leaders: If you're not an accountable leader, when things are going well, you hold up the mirror side of the one-way glass and think to yourself, "Looking good! I'm doing a great job! Just look at my numbers!"

However, when things aren't going so well, that same manager will turn the one-way glass from the mirror to the glass side, looking out to see who – or what – they can blame. They may say, "Well, the market conditions have gone sour," or, "What can you expect when all of my people are idiots! I told them how to do it 10 times and they still don't get it!"

Truly evolved leaders do just the opposite. When things are going well and profits are up, they look through the glass to see whom they can praise and reward. However, when things aren't going well, the first thing they do is look at the mirror side and say,

"How did I fail to communicate that expectation clearly?" or "How can I change the way I communicate the results I expect?"

When Things Go Wrong – Questions to Ask:

1. Where did I fail to communicate clear expectations?

2. Who did I forget to include in initial discussions?

3. What could I have done better or differently that may have resulted in a more favorable outcome?

These same leaders work on themselves all of the time, improving their accountability and modeling the very actions and attitudes they want to see in everyone on their team. In other words, accountable leaders pour their energy into improving what they can control rather than into what they *cannot* ultimately control. You can control yourself and your actions ... you cannot control others.

The challenge is that when somebody on your team or a customer or a supplier is demonstrating low-accountability behaviors, it's easy to get distracted by that and focus on them instead of yourself.

We must first focus on a change within ourselves to create the possibility of change in others.

How to Invite Accountability

One effective way to invite accountability in your personal or professional life is to create accountability partners ... people you invite to hold you accountable for specific tasks.

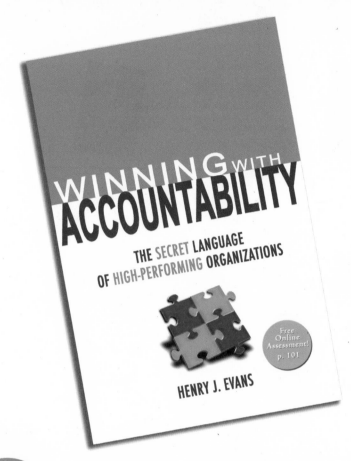

WINNING with **ACCOUNTABILITY**

THE SECRET LANGUAGE OF HIGH-PERFORMING ORGANIZATIONS

Free Online Assessment! p. 101

HENRY J. EVANS

3 **Easy Ways to Order Copies for Your Management Team!**

1. Complete the order form on back and fax to 972-274-2884

2. Visit www.CornerStoneLeadership.com

3. Call 1-888-789-LEAD (5323)

CornerStone
Leadership Institute

Gullible's Travels
Entertaining, enlightening and insightful, this hour-long read prepares people at every level to lead through life's jungle ... and, at the same time, sparks positive ideas to use in leadership roles. Learning from Gullible provides a positive example for your team to become more effective and productive as it makes its way to success. **$14.95**

Leadership Energy (E=mc provides a step-by-step strategy to access your organization's energy reservoir and, through the use of this energy, accelerate your organizatic to the next level. As you read, you'll discover Synchronization, Speed, Communication, Custome Focus, and Integrity – five vital energy conductors to help you energize your team, customers, and profits. **$14.95**

Winning with Accountability
The key to sustained organizational success is accountability – the process of transferring strategies into reality.

This book will provide your organization a roadmap on how to win with accountability. The principles are universal and will work in your organization beginning today! **$14.95**

The Best Leadership Advice I Ever Got is a compilation of 75 CEOs, presidents, professors, politicians and religious leaders describing the best advice they received that helped them become effective leaders! **$14.95**

Who's in the Driver's Seat? Using Spirit to Lead Successfully presents a revolutionary way for leaders to switch on these switched-off employees. Read this book and apply each easy-to-follow lesson ... whether you read one chapter at a time or the entire book in one sitting, the results will be mind-boggling! **$14.95**

7 Moments ... That Defin Excellent Leaders The difference between averag and excellent can be foun in moments ... literally. These moments shape th leaders we are and the leaders we will become. Seize the moment to reac and apply, and you will be one step closer to leadership excellence! **$14.95**

Sticking to It: The Art of Adherence offers practical steps to help you consistently execute your plans. Read it and WIN! **$9.95**

Listen Up, Leader! Ever wonder what employees think about their leaders? This book tells you the seven characteristics of leadership that people will follow. **$9.95**

Visit **www.CornerStoneLeadership.com** for additional books and resources.

Leadership Made Simple: Practical Solutions to Your Greatest Management Challenges is a practical, easy-to-use guide that can produce immediate, tangible, real-world results. It will reshape your culture and dramatically improve every level of performance.
$14.95

Monday Morning Mentoring is an expanded and enhanced hard cover version of best-selling *Monday Morning Leadership*. It includes new sessions on how to deal with change and constructive feedback.
$19.95

Monday Morning Leadership for Women is an inspirational story about a manager and her mentor. It provides insights and wisdom for dealing with leadership issues that are unique to women. **$14.95**

Birdies, Pars & Bogeys: Leadership Lessons from the Links is an excellent gift for the golfing executive. Zig Ziglar praises it as "concise, precise, insightful, inspirational, informative." **$14.95**

Leadership Courage identifies 11 acts of courage required for effective leadership and provides practical steps on how to become a courageous leader.
$14.95

The Leadership Secrets of Santa Claus helps your team accomplish "big things" by giving employees clear goals, solid accountabilities, feedback, coaching, and recognition in your "workshop." **$14.95**

Leadership ER is a powerful story that shares valuable insights on how to achieve and maintain personal health, business health and the critical balance between the two.
$14.95

The Nature of Excellence Daily Inspiration includes an important attribute of excellence and a meaningful quotation. Perfect for office desks, school and home countertops. A great gift or motivational reward.
$15.95

NEW

One of each of the items shown here are included in the *Accelerate Powerful Leadership* Package!

☑ YES! Please send me extra copies of *Winning with Accountability!*
1-30 copies $14.95   31-99 copies $13.95   100+ copies $12.95

Winning with Accountability   copies X _____ = $ _____   _____

Additional Leadership Development Resources

Accelerate Powerful Leadership Package   _____ pack(s) X $199.95   = $ _____
(Includes all items shown inside.)

Other Books

_____   _____ copies X _____   = $ _____

_____   _____ copies X _____   = $ _____

_____   _____ copies X _____   = $ _____

Shipping & Handling $ _____

Subtotal $ _____

Sales Tax (8.25%-TX Only) $ _____

Total (U.S. Dollars Only)   **$** _____

Shipping and Handling Charges

Total $ Amount	Up to $49	$50-$99	$100-$249	$250-$1199	$1200-$2999	$3000+
Charge	$7	$9	$16	$30	$80	$125

Name _____ Job Title _____

Organization _____ Phone_____

Shipping Address _____ Fax _____

Billing Address _____ E-mail_____
                                                                (required when ordering PowerPoint® Presentation)
City _____ State _____ ZIP _____

❑ Please invoice (Orders over $200) Purchase Order Number (if applicable)_____

Charge Your Order: ❑ MasterCard   ❑ Visa   ❑ American Express

Credit Card Number _____ Exp. Date _____

Signature_____

❑ Check Enclosed (Payable to: CornerStone Leadership)

Fax 972.274.2884
Phone 888.789.5323   www.**CornerStoneLeadership**.com   **P.O. Box 764087**
Dallas, TX 75376

An example of a personal commitment may be that you've put on an extra 5 or 10 pounds and you've noticed your energy level is way down. So, you start a diet. If you are reading this book, you are probably a self-motivated person and you will probably lose some weight. At the same time, you also know that an accountability partner will increase your chances of success. You invite a friend or co-worker to hold you accountable for your commitment.

You'll say to your accountability partner, "I'm trying to work on my weight. I'm eating a low-fat diet and I'm exercising three days a week for one hour each day. I've set my goal at 5 pounds per month for the next two months and I'd like you to check in with me on my progress on September 9. That will help me keep my commitment to lose this extra 10 pounds."

As you are imagining this, do a quick gut check. Can you *feel* the difference between making a commitment to yourself and, in contrast, making the same commitment to an accountability partner?

Your accountability partner may then invite you do to the same. "Hey, I've started a new diet and exercise regimen, too. Let's check each other's progress on the 15th and again on the 30th for the next two months."

Your accountability partner may hold you accountable for your commitment in one of two ways. The first – through formal follow-through, in which they say, "Well, did you do it? Did you lose those 5 pounds this month?" Or, they can help you be accountable for your commitment by periodically saying, "I know you're working on losing 5 pounds this month. How's it going?" This is proactive accountability.

Accountability partners are also valuable in holding us accountable for our business commitments.

You and Ron have been co-workers for five years. You respect his values and his work ethic. You say, "Nobody knows this, Ron, but I want to put together two 3-year cash forecasts – one with us opening a plant in China and one without. I think this would be useful for the company to have if it was completed by Oct. 23. Now that you know I have to do this by Oct. 23, which is five weeks from now, when will you follow up with me to see how I'm doing?"

If Ron is a superstar partner, he'll say, "I'll follow up with you weekly," when he agrees to be your accountability partner. If Ron's a superstar accountability partner, he'll also take this next step: "Henry, I know you're working on those two 3-year cash forecasts. How can I support you on your project?"

Here's one more way to invite accountability: Remember when I wanted to read my new martial arts magazine and my assistant reminded me of the project that needed to be completed? Perhaps an encouraging response would have been, "Thank you, Aela. You're helping me stay on task and moving us toward our goal."

By thanking my assistant when she reminded me to get back to my commitment and put away the new martial arts magazine, I invited her to continue holding me accountable by creating a level of comfort in which she can provide these reminders in the future.

Summary:

1. Building a Culture of Accountability requires time, patience and vision … and begins with you.

2. People are watching everything you do. You are always leading one direction or another.

3. First, focus on yourself when determining what might have gone wrong.

4. Ask yourself: Did I communicate clear expectations? Did I include the right people in initial discussions? What could I have done better?

5. Create accountability partners … people you invite to hold you accountable for specific tasks.

What Accountability Partners Sound Like:

✦ I know you are working on "X." How's it going?

✦ You asked me to check in on your progress around project "X." What do I have permission to do if you resist the follow-up?

✦ What are the results so far around project "X"?

THE LANGUAGE OF ACCOUNTABILITY

Nine-tenths of life's serious controversies
come from misunderstanding.
Louis Brandeis

Traditionally, language is perceived to be the structure of how messages are sent and received. However, language actually achieves more by stimulating opinions and creating emotional responses.

For example, there's a new restaurant in town … and the people you work with are raving about the food. Even before you set foot in that restaurant or have lifted that first forkful of food, you now have an opinion. You have positive emotions about that restaurant, simply because you've heard language like "great food," "ambience" and "the best I've ever had."

We use language all of the time, either as a transmitter of our thoughts and information or as a receiver of others' thoughts and information. Since you use language anyway, why not use it in an intentional way to get or achieve what you want?

In creating a high-accountability culture, the appropriate language will elevate performance and improve your communication efficiency. Your dialogue will be fast, powerful and complete.

The Four Stages of Language Development

Accountability language is real. It is visible and palpable, and there is a process to learning and using it to help you achieve positive results.

Learning the Language of Accountability is similar to how human beings learn their native language. Toddlers, for example, hear their parents using language. At some point in their development, toddlers may even mimic the sounds their parents are using, even though they don't know the words or understand the meaning.

Eventually, these little ones begin to connect meanings to words, learn to string them together into sentences and then begin using language to convey their needs or get what they want. That's one way we learned our native language.

Now, suppose your native language is English and you're sitting in an airport. The couple next to you is speaking Portuguese, a language you've never heard before.

Several weeks later, you're watching a Portuguese movie with English subtitles and you immediately recognize this as the language the couple had been speaking at the airport.

Because you're a lifelong learner and you are interested in foreign languages, you decide to sign up for a Portuguese course at the local college. By the end of the semester, you have a basic understanding of close to 100 vocabulary words. As you continue to read, study and listen to Portuguese, before long, not only can you understand spoken Portuguese, but you are also beginning to speak it yourself.

The learning process of developing organizational accountability language is very similar to learning a new language. The same four phases of language learning – hearing, recognizing, understanding and speaking – apply.

The Four Steps of Learning a New Language

1. Hearing

2. Recognizing

3. Understanding

4. Speaking – this is when organizational change begins

In this chapter, you will discover that as you apply the Language of Accountability, you will model it for your team and others you work with. Eventually, it will be a natural process. Your accountability culture begins … not with the organization changing as a whole but, instead, with the language that you as an individual choose to use. It is through individual change that organizational change occurs and the change begins with you!

Accountability Gaps and How They Grow

You will also discover that high-accountability cultures are something you can see.

To illustrate this, let's take a professional basketball player, a star of the NBA who, at one time in his career, declared, "I'm not a role model. Parents should be role models."

We're not using his name here because that was a goofy thing for any star athlete to say. Because, despite what he thought, there were thousands of children admiring that NBA star, wearing his jersey number, and shooting baskets until dark to become just like him. In the context of accountability, even though he was a top scorer and exciting to watch on the court, you could see that athlete wasn't a star in the Culture of Accountability.

Now, let's turn the dial to 1993 and the confrontation at the Mt. Carmel Complex of the Branch Davidians led by David Koresh in Waco, Texas.

On April 19, 1993, Attorney General Janet Reno gave the FBI permission to flush the Davidians out of their residence, using tanks to smash holes in the walls of the building and then spraying tear gas into the residence. Agents then fired more than 350 "ferret" grenades into the building, but none of the Davidians obeyed the FBI's command to exit the residence. A fire then broke out and 76 Davidians, including 27 children, perished.

As word of the confrontation and resulting deaths made the evening news, Janet Reno stepped up to the microphone at a White House press conference. "I made the decision," she said. "I'm accountable. The buck stops with me." Her words were notable – and noticeable – because you rarely hear politicians speak this way. At that time, she was the first female U.S. attorney general and fairly new to her job. Yet, in the face of a tragic and controversial situation, she stepped forward and was accountable. You could see that Janet Reno was exhibiting an accountability culture that was the model for her entire organization.

So, what does a high-accountability culture look like? Accountability cultures do not happen overnight. The culture evolves from one person or event to the next. One common denominator is that **in accountability cultures, everyone holds each other accountable for their commitments in a positive and productive manner.**

Earlier, we asked if you had ever had a relationship or a project fail. If you answered, "Yes," chances are high that failure occurred because specificity was missing at the front end and expectations weren't clear. That relationship or that project failed because there were "accountability gaps."

Accountability gaps are like potholes in a road. The gaps are holes that need to be filled quickly with specificity before greater damage is done. Just like potholes in the road need to be filled quickly with paving materials before the holes become so large that they damage the cars on the road, an "accountability gap" exists when specificity is missing.

Let's take poor Max, who was hired by a large company. His boss told him, "Max, we're glad to have you on the team, and as long as you do a good job, your employment with us is solid." Unfortunately, his boss didn't tell Max, specifically, what a good job looked like (count this as one pothole). When Max headed the team for a major project, the boss said, "Get that final report to me as soon as you can." Once again, did that mean tomorrow or next week? Max did his best but the report was several days tardy in his boss's eyes (another pothole).

By the time Max was fired, his tenure was rutted with potholes, lacking specificity and becoming deeper and causing more damage as the weeks and months went by.

Max failed because there was specificity missing in every expectation and assignment. Nothing was clearly stated at the front end ... and when there's no specificity on the front end, Max was set up to fail.

But, let's not throw Max's boss under the bus just yet. Max made a big mistake, as well. He "assumed" he knew what the boss meant when he was told to "do a good job" and to get the report completed "as soon as you can." Assumptions dig deep potholes and are great contributors to accountability gaps leading to a failed project or relationship ... and these lead to bad feelings, which become a vicious cycle of dysfunction.

Accountability is a two-way street. If you complete a task that was not specific and someone is disappointed in your work, you are the one who is considered unreliable. You're past the point of no return. It's too late for expectations. It's a "gotcha" of the worst kind in every sense.

It is the role of both the sender and the receiver of the information to make sure all the potholes are filled before the task begins.

The Glossary of Failure

Language used to forecast relationship or project failure is called the "Glossary of Failure." It's ambiguous, lack's specificity and will assuredly lead to disappointment, failure and bad feelings. Ambiguity and generalizations lead to disappointment.

Here's a good example. If you ask three people what "ASAP" means to them, you'll probably get three different answers as to the specific timeframe in which "ASAP" is carried out.

Now, let's say I'm promising an external customer a new copier and I'm relying on you to complete the service contract. You tell me you'll get it to the customer ASAP – an ambiguous answer. How can I make a real delivery commitment to that customer?

Or, what about the ambiguous "I'll get right on it"? Do you mean you'll do the task immediately ... or as soon as you finish reading your e-mails ... or after you've had lunch? When is "right on it"?

Don't confuse the Glossary of Failure with lack of intention. Sometimes, "I'll get right on it," means that they have great intention and, in fact, really intend to complete the project. You don't want to dampen their enthusiasm but you do wish to clarify the commitment.

Intentions can't be measured. The employee who promised to "get right on it" may have had no intention of getting to your project this afternoon, the next day or even this week. That's not lack of accountability. That's grounds for termination due to lack of interest.

Suppose someone says they are going to have a report "by the end of the day." So, what's "the end of the day" for you? Is it 5 p.m.? Is it your bedtime? Or, does the end of the day come when the clock strikes midnight? Who knows and how can the person be held accountable for an ambiguous answer?

If you're working with branch offices around the country or around the globe, the "end of the day" occurs at many different times. Let's say you're working on the East Coast and someone on the West Coast promises a completed task by the end of the day. Is that Eastern Standard Time or Pacific Time? Is it at 5 p.m. on your coast or 5 p.m. on their coast?

Even things that seem obvious can be a part of the Glossary of Failure. What about a promise to complete a project by the end of the year? If your corporation works on a fiscal year, that could be August or September or October. If it works on a calendar year, it's December – but is it the first of December or the last day of December?

As you are probably observing, these types of ambiguities are all part of the Glossary of Failure ... and every one of these vague phrases increases the chances of relationship or project failure.

Here are some of the biggest offenders from the Glossary of Failure:

✦ Soon

✦ ASAP

✦ Right away

✦ I'll get right on it!

✦ The end of the day/week/month/year

✦ Later

✦ Try

✦ Should

✦ Best

✦ Might

✦ By the "next time" we meet

✦ We

So what can you do to neutralize this ambiguity? Begin using the language of specificity.

High-Accountability Language

The opposite of the Glossary of Failure is the Language of Specificity.

Instead of saying, "I'll have this report on your desk ASAP," you say, "I'll have that report on your desk by 1 p.m. this afternoon."

Rather than saying, "We'll have the project completed by the end of the day," tell your counterpart, "I'll have it wrapped up by Tuesday, June 13th at 10 a.m., your time."

Like the three most important rules of real estate are "location, location, location," **the three most important rules in creating an accountability culture are "specificity, specificity, specificity."**

Practice making commitments, using the Language of Accountability by saying, "I will do it on 'X' date at 'X' time."

The Language of Specificity includes:

- ✦ What date and time should I follow up with you to make sure the loop is closed?
- ✦ Who owns it?
- ✦ I own it!
- ✦ Will (e.g., "I will' in lieu of "try," "should," or "might.")
- ✦ Here's what it will look like when it is completed.

Using the Language of Specificity will increase accountability and strengthen the accountability culture within your organization.

As you practice avoiding the Glossary of Failure and increase your mastery of the Language of Specificity, you'll see your performance increase. High-performing leaders are skilled at listening for ambiguity in language and replacing it with specificity.

Remember the four steps of acquiring new language – hearing, recognizing, understanding and speaking? You will experience this same sequence as you become highly skilled at listening for specificity.

You'll also move through these same four phases as you begin using the Language of Specificity when asking for – and making – commitments and building a Culture of Accountability within your organization.

State It Once

A Culture of Accountability also helps eliminate redundancy.

Focusing solely on a problem and not on the solution wastes resources on redundancy. Everyone knows what the problem is … your energy and resources need to be focused on solving the problem. It may be productive to voice the problem once, but then it is time to move the momentum toward a solution to improve our position. Redundancy is not in many job descriptions.

A good example of the momentum of leadership would be a conversation like this:

Manager: "I've noticed Phil isn't coming through with his assignments on time … and it's getting to be a real problem for me."

You: "I've also noticed that, too. What's causing it? Where have we failed to set specific timelines and expectations?"

In pointing out that the failure may be on leadership's shoulders, you're looking into the mirror to find solutions.

State the problem once, eliminate redundancy, and move toward the solution.

Reversing Momentum

Language momentum can be reversed … from any person in the organization.

Here's an example:

In 1975, a movie about a mammoth killer shark was filmed. The title – *Jaws*.

After this shark has eaten a few tourists, a town meeting is called where the mayor, the chief of police, the city council and some influential business owners are all in attendance.

Many see no other option but to close the local beaches to fend off any more attacks and more bad publicity. However, businesses in the community want to leave them open. This is the "high" season for tourists and closing the beaches now will bankrupt most of the community.

The argument goes back and forth between the two factions for several minutes. No ground is gained and neither of the two sides is willing to give an inch or find a compromise. The meeting is at a stalemate. The upper echelon of the town's organizational chart is stuck in the problem. The arguing is getting louder and louder.

Then, the gut-wrenching sound of nails being dragged down the blackboard interrupts the argument. Suddenly the room is silent and necks are craned to see a simple fisherman sitting at the back of the room near the blackboard. When he has the room's attention, he quietly offers, "I can kill that fish for $6,000."

That pronouncement, made by the somewhat obscure and low-profile fisherman (who was probably not on anybody's org chart), changed the entire momentum of the meeting … and also changed the direction and focus of an entire town. The simple fisherman had taken on the leadership role, and from that point forward, the town's momentum had shifted to assembling the team that would kill that shark!

That's the way it can work in any situation. It's the leader's job to reverse the momentum of negative interactions – and anyone can be the leader regardless of their position on the organizational chart. You can reverse the momentum by applying your skills and energy toward a new, positive outcome. When a conversation is in the past (with celebrations as an exception) you are probably focused on a "problem" or, perhaps, assigning blame. However, by changing the momentum and focusing the dialogue on the future, you are now working on a "plan."

In short, you have the power to identify Accountability Gaps during interactions and fill them with Specificity. You have the power to identify when an interaction is "going negative" and reverse the momentum so that everyone involved in the interaction benefits!

Wipe out the Glossary of Failure within your team or your organization … use the Language of Specificity!

In the next four chapters, we will examine the four components of an accountability dialogue. This is where you learn to apply the language principles you just read. By including these Four Pieces of the Accountability Puzzle in our language, we increase individual and organizational performance!

Summary:

1. A Culture of Accountability is a culture where all team members hold each other accountable for their commitments in a positive and productive manner.

2. "Potholes" occur when specificity of language is missing, particularly in making commitments. These potholes can be filled in with specific and accountable information.

3. The Glossary of Failure contains the language we use that forecasts relationship or project failure. It's ambiguous, lacks specificity and will assuredly lead to disappointment, failure and bad feelings.

4. The opposite of the Glossary of Failure is the Language of Accountability ... the Language of Specificity.

5. It is the leader's job to reverse the momentum of negative interactions – and anyone can be the leader.

I Can See Clearly Now

Clear Expectation

Without clear expectations, people are being paid to guess.

had been observing a client for several days. Our shared goal was to move the organization into a high-accountability culture. On my second day of consulting with this corporation, I was invited to attend a meeting where the board was welcoming Dave, their new executive vice president of marketing, to his first meeting with the company.

When it came time for the CEO to welcome Dave onboard, he began with these words:

"We're glad to have you with us and look forward to working with you. You'll be in charge of our next international client conference, and we're all counting on you. We want this next conference to be the best one we've ever had."

And, with that, the CEO took his seat, the meeting continued to its conclusion and everyone left the room.

Later that afternoon, the CEO sat across his desk from me and asked, "Well, how do you think I did?"

My response was probably not the one he wanted to hear. "I feel that your intention was to give him both clear direction and encouragement. I'm not convinced we accomplished those objectives. He may know more than I do, but I didn't have the least idea what you expected," I said, "and since I'd never attended an international client conference, I couldn't picture what the 'best one we've ever had' even looked like."

His expression said it all. He was surprised … and probably disappointed he hadn't done a better job of clarifying his expectations.

Then I shared what psychologists have determined about how we can communicate our requests with more clarity. It's called "visual association," which means providing a picture of what you're requesting.

Creating Clarity

The CEO and I worked on the concept of creating clarity for a little less than an hour and then he asked the new EVP to come to his office. He asked me to remain so I would be able to offer additional feedback.

"I don't think I did a very good job of telling you what I wanted to come from our next international client conference," the CEO said, "so let me try again."

The new EVP looked relieved, nodded and settled back in his chair.

"As you may know, we're planning to hold our next international client conference on August 29, at the Venetian Hotel in Las Vegas," he said.

The EVP nodded in agreement.

"We're going to have a cocktail hour in the Venetian's ballroom, beginning at 6 p.m. the evening before the conference," the CEO continued. "I'm going to walk into the ballroom at 6:15 p.m. and when I do, I want to see 150 smiling customers, representing 20 different client organizations. I also want them to be holding a beverage, chatting and enjoying themselves."

The CEO paused and the EVP nodded again, more enthusiastically than the first time.

"Can you see that, Dave?" the CEO asked.

Dave answered affirmatively.

At the end of their conversation, Dave stood and expressed his appreciation for the clarification.

After the new EVP left the office, the CEO turned to me. "Well, how did I do this time?"

"Fantastic! Passed with flying colors," I said. "You gave Dave a detailed picture of how 'the best conference ever' would begin. He got it and now he has a clear picture of your expectation."

> ## To Remodel a Situation
> Take responsibility, describe a desired outcome, and reflect understanding by asking for reflection from the other person.

Bridging the Accountability Gap with Clear Expectations

A clear expectation is something that is visual, can be measured and is clearly understood by both the person making the request and the person receiving the request. When our expectations are clear, people know what they're working toward. With unclear expectations, we're actually paying people to guess.

Communicating your expectations with clarity is the first step in bridging accountability gaps.

Unclear expectations are the norm in organizations around the world. The main reason why people do not live up to other's expectations is because they do not know what the expectations are. They mentally "see" a different result and assume their perspective and interpretation are correct.

Here are some common examples of assuming perspectives: "I thought it was a good movie, so other people will, too." Or, "I think this restaurant is a good place to have dinner, so other people will, too."

Like the CEO I mentioned at the beginning of this chapter, by checking in and asking for reflection from others, we'll find out if the expectation is clear. Remember, it's what other people see, not what we said.

THE ACCOUNTABILITY PUZZLE

Truly accountable actions often seem like a big puzzle – The Accountability Puzzle.

The Accountability Puzzle is a model that requires four pieces to create accountable dialogue and actions. When you have these four components imbedded in requests that you make of others, and in commitments that you make to others, individual and organizational performance improve. By knowing and understanding each piece, you can start having more productive and accountable dialogues immediately. Your requests will involve more accountability and you will be able to listen for more accountable responses.

Putting all four pieces to this Accountability Puzzle together works!

The puzzle fits together perfectly but the pieces need to be put in order. The first step follows.

Clear Expectation – The First Piece of the Accountability Puzzle

Every request you make should include a crystal-clear result of your expectation. Your best friend, spouse or child should be able to visualize the outcome before they begin working toward it.

If your expectation is not clearly expressed and if they cannot get a picture of what you want, you cannot expect them to read your mind and deliver the results you expect. Everyone is more effective and efficient when they have a clear vision and a clear idea of what's expected.

An unclear expectation is like asking a teenager, "Hey, would you spend some time this afternoon cleaning up my car?"

The request hasn't been clearly expressed and the teenager can't possibly visualize what you're asking him or her to do. They will do exactly what they want to do ... and it will probably not even closely resemble your expectations.

But what if you said, "I'd like you to clean the car this afternoon ... and I'd like for you to do it well enough for me to see my reflection in the finish." The expectation is clear and they now have a goal and vision of what you expect.

The benefit of expressing a request so the listener will have a visual concept of what you expect creates a clear focus for one or more other people. This results in better retention, more efficiency and better use of resources — yours and theirs.

Research at universities from California to the East Coast continues to ratify this same theory — a visual image of a concept encourages better memory ... of a story, a task or a request.

Clarity in the Language of Accountability

How do we know if our expectation is clear? One tool that will help is a self-assessment using the acronym **S.M.A.R.T.E.R.** This tool makes certain our expectation is specific, measurable, attainable, results-oriented, trackable, ethical and recorded.

S.M.A.R.T.E.R. will become a filter for requests of others *before* you make them. Ask yourself, "Does my request meet all of the S.M.A.R.T.E.R requirements?" By using this tool, we are thoughtful enough to carry out due diligence in order to see if the request we're making is reasonable.

Each step is important and each question must be answered positively.

Specific – Have I described and provided a visual of the behaviors and deadlines required for good job performance?

Measurable – Can my request be measured? Does it have a clearly defined completion point? When it's all said and done, can you actually measure if the request was done? If you make the request, "Go out and increase sales," that's not measurable. If you say, instead, "Go out and sell $1M to new customers this month," that's measurable! It has a clearly defined completion point.

Attainable – Is it realistic for this person or this team to achieve and accomplish my request within the stated guidelines? Are they capable? Do they have the right resources to accomplish the expected outcome?

Results-Oriented – Does this request move us closer to our objective? It's possible to make a request that doesn't get us anywhere near where we need to be. We don't want tasks that simply cause us to work. We want tasks that cause us to get change accomplished.

Trackable – What milestones will ensure that we are on the right track to accomplish our goals? How will we measure performance milestones during the effort?

Ethical – Is the request legal, moral and ethical? Does what you're doing align with organizational and personal values? Know what your ethics are and make sure your requests align with these same values.

Recorded – Is there a record or a second person who knows about the request or the effort? There should be a point of reference, something people can look to for guidance, aside from the originator.

Once you have positively answered each of the S.M.A.R.T.E.R. questions, then you can move forward and make your request. At the end of the request, ask your team for reflection. You're not asking the listener/receiver to repeat your request verbatim. Instead, you invite them to express what they heard using questions such as, "What does what I just said mean to you?" or "I explained this to the best of my ability but what did you actually hear?" or "What does this look like to you when it's done?"

If you embrace the philosophy that *other people's perceptions equal your reality*, then measurement of how clearly you've communicated is reflected in how people hear you.

The S.M.A.R.T.E.R. self-assessment will ensure that you and your team are communicating thoughtful, accountable requests leading to desired outcomes.

Here are some observations based on my experiences:

✦ People deal with you based on what they think of you, not what you think about yourself.

✦ Since two of us can see the same movie at the same time and each hold different opinions about it, both opinions are valid and true. The same goes for how you may be perceived by others. Take their input as "data."

Data = Information

Information = Power
(Now you can do something about it.)

If you sense a miscommunication, and before you assign blame to others, first check yourself to make sure you're providing clear expectations every step of the way. Of course, it may be the other person, but look before you jump to conclusions.

In a perfect world, these concepts would cause everyone around you to fulfill their commitments to you, as you intended, all of the time. Unfortunately, our world's not perfect, and there will be people who aren't consistently meeting your expectations. If you've provided a clear and visual expectation and someone isn't producing the results you expected, here are two ways to respond to this situation:

1. **Use past tense** – "I'm just curious. What did it mean when you said _____ ?" As an example, "Erika, my perception is that this is the third time you've stood me up for lunch … so I'm just curious. What did it mean when you said you'd meet me for lunch today at noon?" You are allowing the person to provide you their perception of your expectation.

This is the softer of the two approaches. The next response will escalate the conversation:

2. **Use future tense** – "What should I expect the next time you promise to _____?" An example would be, "Erika, I feel like I'm losing confidence in you. I'm losing confidence because the last three times you promised to meet me for lunch, you didn't show up. Based on my experience, what should my expectation be the next time you make this promise?"

   Another variation: "You said you'll meet me for lunch tomorrow. What should my expectation be?"

In any business or personal relationship, there's a point where broken commitments put the relationship in jeopardy. Losing trust will destroy relationships and, in order to create a Culture of Accountability, we think these situations need to be addressed, not destructively but overtly.

Once you've mastered clarity, you will be using the Language of Accountability ... an essential first step. In the next chapter, we will introduce the second piece of the Accountability Puzzle: *specificity*.

Summary:

1. The first piece of the Accountability Puzzle is clarity. When we make a request with clear expectations we create a visual representation that all parties can see. Your team will be motivated, focused and working on the right thing.

2. If specificity is missing in your request, accountability gaps are created.

3. The first step in bridging these accountability gaps is setting clear, visual expectations, replacing ambiguity with specificity.

4. Do not confuse "accountability" with "consequences." They are related ... and different. Consequences should simply be stated as part of setting clear expectations. By communicating consequences as part of the front-loaded clear expectation, we have created accountability!

It's Time to Get Specific

Specific
Date & Tme

Timing is everything in a Culture of Accountability.

At one time, most people lived in a close, small circle. Everyone in your family, everyone you knew and everything you did occurred in one small area. Whenever you purchased something or made a promise to do a job or committed to do something for someone, these agreements were usually made in the same town ... and sealed with a handshake.

In those days, you could say, "Be home by dark," and that was about as specific as you needed to be in terms of time … because everyone knew when "dark" occurred and it was the same for everyone.

But, that was then. This is now.

Specificity, Specificity, Specificity

In today's business environment, things have changed … and many of these changes are due to the expanding opportunities to work with global clients and partners. With this change comes a greater need for time specificity, which is the second piece of the Accountability Puzzle.

Today's business environment dictates that we need to adjust some of our common, not-so-clear phrases. These adjustments are especially critical in terms of time specificity. In other words, we need to be more specific … about the date, the time and the time zone.

Suppose, for example, my counterpart in Portugal tells me, "I'll have that first quarter report to you by the end of the day today."

You may have already figured out my next question to my counterpart. "When is the end of the day? What do you mean? Is it the end of the day for me personally, for my branch, for my region or is it your end of the day?" In Portugal, which is five hours ahead of U.S. Eastern Standard Time, their end of the day would come five hours ahead of yours – that is, if you believe the end of the day occurs at 5 p.m.

However, some people see the "end of the day" as when they go to bed every night, which could range from 8 p.m. to 1 a.m., depending on sleep habits.

Someone saying, "I'll have the report to you by the end of the day" is not time specific enough to have meaning in a Culture of Accountability.

That's why the second piece of the Accountability Puzzle is a specific date, time and time zone. For example, instead of saying, "I'll get this to you in New York next week," using the Accountability Method, you'll say, "You will have this on your desk by next Friday, December 20th at 3 p.m. EST."

Because this commitment is so concise and so clear, it's difficult to misinterpret that promise. **As specificity goes up, miscommunication goes down.** But something else also occurs. Those accustomed to making ambiguous commitments – without time specificity – also will see their comfort level go down as their wiggle room becomes less and less.

As you already may realize, time specificity – including the date, time and time zone – has become more and more important because our circle of communications now includes global audiences. Time specificity means we must speak to everyone – particularly those in other time zones – in terms of their specific dates and times.

Specificity: Intellectually Simple – Behaviorally Complex

The concept of accountability is intellectually simple but behaviorally complex? Here is a good example of what happens when a commitment lacks the time specificity piece of the Accountability Puzzle.

About a year ago, I was going to be in New Mexico on business. On Wednesday, June 18, the week previous to my appointment in New Mexico, I made a call to my family in Albuquerque and set up a time to have dinner with them on Friday of the following week. That date would have been June 27, but I didn't specify that.

We discussed restaurants we liked and made a date to meet at a certain restaurant at 6 p.m. "that" Friday we had discussed.

Somehow, my mother assumed I was going to be in Albuquerque the same week of my call and, as a result, two days later, when Friday, June 20, rolled around, my family went to the restaurant and waited for me ... and waited ... and waited.

I had just been through a very demanding week, so on that same Friday, I went home, shut off my phone and treated myself to a movie. Unbeknownst to me, my family in Albuquerque was waiting for me at the restaurant. When it got to be 6:30 and then 7 p.m., they started calling, trying my cell phone – which was off – and then my home phone, which also was unplugged. I was happily watching a movie that I'd been wanting to see.

The next morning, when I turned my phone on, I had messages, escalating in urgency ... from my parents, my assistant, team members in the company and several friends because my mother had begun contacting them. When I hadn't shown up at the restaurant in Albuquerque, and they couldn't reach me by phone, my family had begun looking for my body. All parties involved agreed that based on my history of being reliable and accountable to my commitments, if I had not shown up, without even calling, I could be in real trouble.

This situation was created by an unfortunate accountability gap – and one I hadn't realized would occur just by not emphasizing the date. I had opened the door for a panic attack for everyone else –

all because I hadn't used a specific date … resulting in my mother being really emotionally traumatized.

Had I used a specific date rather than just saying, "see you *next* Friday," the entire situation would have been avoided. Had my mother requested specificity in our agreement by stating the date, we also would have avoided the situation.

What is it they say about making assumptions?

Specific and Visible

Time specificity improves productivity, morale and results. It is a vital part of creating high-accountability cultures. If we've been given a specific date and time, we can look at our calendars – and once we see the date and time, our minds create a visual interpretation and our retention doubles.

When you speak in specific dates and times, you're actually causing the people who are listening to create a visual picture. When they get that visual picture, they will better retain what is being said.

For instance, let's say you borrowed some money from me a few weeks ago … and you tell me, "I'm going to pay you back next week."

With that commitment, I have no visual picture.

But, what if you said, "I'm going to pay back the money I owe you with a personal check on March 3, at 3 p.m. Pacific Time." Now that you've made the commitment using time specificity as well as other specific details, I can see it on my calendar. My retention rate doubles because I have a visual.

In addition, when someone is making a commitment, if you ask them to speak it with a specific date and time, they will be more likely to remember their own commitment.

When you include a date, time and time zone, there's no question about when this commitment is due. It cannot be reasonably interpreted any other way.

Deadlines vs. Timelines

What is the difference between deadlines and timelines – and which works best in a Culture of Accountability?

In school – and probably for the biggest part of our lives – we've learned when the work was supposed to be done. That's a deadline. So, if a book report was due Monday at 8:30 a.m., many of us were rushing to complete our homework that morning and doing it in a way that probably wasn't our best work, right?

A timeline, on the other hand, is when we actually do the work.

For example, let's suppose we are having a strategic planning meeting for a client. In our proposal, we committed to 30 hours of planning time. These aren't evenings and weekends but 30 hours of prime planning time to meet my commitment. Those are the hours when my mind is sharp and focused and when all of my resources are available. I am more productive in two-hour planning blocks, so my time was committed in multiple blocks of two hours.

So, I take 30 hours and create 15 two-hour blocks on my calendar to do this client work. I take these scheduled work "blocks" as seriously as I would meeting with another person. For that reason, I "show up" on time. I am not working on a deadline – I am working on a timeline.

Without proactive, thoughtful timelines, we're probably living in reaction to deadlines … doing Tuesday's work on the way to the office Tuesday morning.

Without timelines, deadlines often put us in a jam. With timelines, deadlines are more easily and readily achieved. Productivity is higher and stress levels are lower.

> **Remember:** A deadline is when work is due. A timeline is when the work gets done. And, in a Culture of Accountability, it's when the work gets done that really counts.

Successful manufacturing, distribution, product development, or major project accomplishment is achieved through the use of timelines. Why wouldn't we apply the same standards of success into an executive's time?

> **TOOL:** Schedule your tasks as meetings on your calendar and start and finish them on time as if other people were involved in the meeting.

One of the biggest sticking points in accountability cultures is managing our time. How many times have you heard someone use the excuse, "I don't have time"?

I hear it regularly. When I ask clients what got in the way of accomplishing something, they might say, "I didn't have time."

That's a hard one to swallow, especially if you realize we all – no matter what our role is at work – have the same exact amount of time, 24/7/365. So it becomes an issue of how we manage our time. And part of being accountable is prioritizing our time around what's most important. This is something that has to be practiced. It takes thought and thoughtfulness to prioritize and allocate time.

So how can you begin?

Look at your calendar … either on Friday before leaving work or Monday before you start your week. Decide what's most important and see how your calendar is – or isn't – aligning with what you say is most important. One way to create this alignment is to list the things you need to do and the amount of time each takes. Then, look at the available time on your calendar and reconcile these two factors.

Most of us can't do everything, and it's a fallacy to think we can. So, we must prioritize what's most important. **We need to know that, at the end of the day, what we *did* get done is more important than what we *didn't* get done.**

Whether we realize it or not, we are prioritizing all of the time. Most people will spend a few minutes every night mentally prioritizing what they want to do the following day. In this process, they are usually putting what's important to them ahead of what may be important to others. Our list may include the following: a conference call, finalizing contracts for the new project, lunch with the EVP or reviewing the last three quarterly reports in preparation for a meeting the next day.

What's not on our list is a performance review for one of our direct reports … a performance review that was due several weeks ago, but "we just haven't had the time," right?

People do what is important to them. You can always see what's truly important to another individual by what they choose to do and how they choose to spend their time.

So, let's go back to that performance review for a moment. While we might view ourselves as being extremely busy, facing time crunch after time crunch, the employee waiting for their performance review might view us as breaking a commitment. In a Culture of Accountability, a broken promise means a lack of integrity resulting in a lack of trust.

Our priorities must be aligned with our commitments.

Once you have mastered imbedding your requests and your commitments with specific dates and times, you are ready to move to the third piece of the puzzle: *ownership*, which is covered in the next chapter.

Summary:

1. The Language of Accountability is specific about dates, times and time zones. It's also realistic when it comes to managing time and aligning priorities with time and resources available.

2. Time specificity, which is vital to creating a Culture of Accountability, works with timelines, not deadlines.

3. Time specificity can protect your integrity.

Tool: Try checking your current commitments (as stated on your calendar) against what you have deemed to be "most important." Make adjustments as necessary.

Ownership

Ownership

Who's in charge here, anyway?

T he third piece of the puzzle focuses on ownership around those objectives within the stated timeframe.

One Task – One Owner

For every action, there should only be one owner ... the one person responsible for a task being performed. You may be saying there's no "I" in team, and tasks are commonly accomplished by teams of people. But my point is this: There are no "teams" in ownership.

There are no teams in ownership.

Teams may perform various actions to complete a project, but there should only be one owner per action. While the team may own the overall outcome, the action that gets us to that outcome should only have one person in charge.

So, if you're the owner of the initiative and the team meets the expectations, give all the praise and credit that you can to your team members. If, however, the team does not perform, you should look in the mirror to find ways you can improve as a leader.

Of course, it's great if a team feels ownership, but we still have to know whom the actual owner is. When there's one owner, it's clear who's in charge, who to bring changes and suggestions to and who the go-to person is. It also eliminates confusion when surprises appear.

For example, you're on a team developing a trade show display for an upcoming convention and Jack is responsible for the outcome. You receive a phone call from a vendor saying he's two days behind schedule in shipping a key part of the display. Since Jack is the owner of the outcome, you know to immediately go to Jack and tell him what the vendor said. Then Jack can decide if he wants to continue working with the tardy vendor or would rather look at other options. The decision can be made immediately and you move forward. Having one owner of the project saves time and eliminates confusion.

The second reason there should be only one owner for every outcome is because if that owner leaves, the organization can easily outline what the successor is responsible for completing. This not only assures progress but also promotes success, no matter what may be happening internally.

If, for example, the owner of the outcome leaves – due to illness, retirement or any other reason – as you are looking to backfill that position, you may want to fill that position against the responsibilities vacated by the owner of the project. This makes recruitment easier and more thoughtful. The transition would be smoother and less stressful.

Like a flock of geese that constantly changes leaders as they fly north or south, teams also can change ownership roles. You can change ownership of an action, but **it must always be clear who the owner is**. Optimally, the best choice for ownership is the person best suited to perform the work with the best experience.

Where the Buck Stops

As a team leader, you take ownership – not only of the outcome but also your circumstances. A declaration of self, so to speak. As leader, the buck stops with you. It may be natural to find yourself blaming others when projects fail or situations degenerate. However, if the buck truly stops at your desk, you have to own the project, even if you delegate every task.

Let's revisit the scenario in Chapter Four about the new EVP of marketing and the client cocktail party in Las Vegas. In that scenario, the EVP is owner of the most successful client conference ever, but he may have delegated every aspect of that project to achieve the final outcome.

He probably delegated invitation design to someone from marketing, and someone from IT was assigned to distribute messages. Someone from the travel department made arrangements for client travel. Someone from accounting is in charge of paying final bills. But on the night of the client cocktail party at 6:15 p.m., the EVP is owner of high-level expectations, while those to whom he delegated the various tasks leading up to this event are owners of the actions that got us to the party.

Ownership may be voluntary or it may be assigned, but in a Culture of Accountability, **ownership must be present at an individual level.**

How do you achieve ownership? How do you have employees take ownership? One way is by modeling (i.e. taking ownership yourself). People follow people more than they follow plans. If you accept ownership, they will accept ownership. If you pass the buck, the buck will be passed again. People follow you, and you have to take ownership to lead them where you want them to follow.

Achieving ownership also happens by asking, "Who's going to own this concept and then each action within it?" How many times have you – or someone else – said, "John's the best person to do this, but he's so overwhelmed, let's give it to Suzy."

Very quickly, you saw ownership move from John – who had the competence but not the time or bandwidth – to Suzy, who has the bandwidth (time) but maybe not John's competence to get the job done well. This could result in the work being completed, but not to the standard you were expecting to deliver.

Competency First, Then Bandwidth

In most cases, ownership should be assigned by competency first and bandwidth second – which is the opposite of how it's usually done. The optimum situation is to have people spending most of their time doing what they are best at doing. When corporations want high performance, they must be continually filtering assignments through competency and then bandwidth filters.

What about the old "Let George do it ... George does everything well"?

If you make decisions solely on competency, it is possible that you will overload your best performers. When capable employees are constantly overwhelmed, that is an indicator of an organizational issue. The issue could be understaffing or you may not have the right people on the team. These are called "operational efficiency issues" and must be addressed before you can create a culture of accountability.

The bottom line is that the organization should be focused on having people doing what they are best at doing most of the time. We're never gonna be perfect. For instance, if Pete is absolutely the best sales closer we have, and we're going to present to the biggest prospect in our history during an economic downturn, his being busy is not a reason for him not to be the guy on that call. His competencies tell us he needs to be the guy on that call. He's our front man. He's the one we want in front of the client.

> When I cross the Sahara Desert,
> I want the most dependable guy to carry the water.
> I don't really care who carries the perfume.

A senior associate in our firm retired after 22 years in the Army. He worked directly for a former secretary of defense for the last 10 of those years. When the Army decided to downsize, the secretary went to him and said, "I'm putting you in charge of this. I want you to be the guy that restructures the U.S. Army and makes us a functional organization at this much smaller size."

He created a simple but effective process ... based on competencies. Since then, he's been asked to work with several high-profile corporations. His very first action is to look at an organization's strategic plan and asks, "Does your organizational chart today support that organizational structure and vision you have for tomorrow?"

The answer is almost always "No."

So the next step is to design an organizational structure that supports the vision, creating a core competency model for each position. His philosophy is to evaluate the skills your people need to have ... and then assess people against those skills. In other words, select owners by competency first and bandwidth second.

If you have a team where every person is of relatively equal competency, then select an owner for a project outcome based on bandwidth. Equal competency throughout a team is a great but rare situation. But if – and only if – that is the situation on your team, then select the owner based on bandwidth.

Once you've modeled and taught ownership – the third piece of the Accountability Puzzle – you'll be ready to move to the fourth piece of the puzzle: *share*.

Summary:

1. Only one person should be the owner of a task. A team cannot own a task.

2. The buck stops with the owner of a project ... even if every task has been delegated.

3. Assign ownership by competency first, bandwidth (time) second.

4. Today's organizational chart should support your vision of tomorrow's organization.

GOING PUBLIC

Share

*Accountability is born when two or more people
know about a commitment.*

Let me set the scene: You've decided to get serious about losing 5 pounds.

Now, compare two different approaches to losing this weight. In Approach #1, you keep your goal to yourself. You struggle in silence to pass up that second helping of potatoes. You try to exercise every chance you get ... and you weigh yourself every day.

In Approach #2, you decide to lose 5 pounds and you tell a friend, "I'm going to lose 5 pounds by August 25th, but I'd like you to check in with me on August 1, just to see how I'm progressing."

Now, contrast how it feels when you tell yourself you're going to lose 5 pounds to how it feels when you tell a friend, "I'm going to lose 5 pounds by August 25, but I want you to check in with me on August 1st."

If you are like most, you can physically feel the difference between making a commitment to yourself and letting someone else know about it and asking them to help you with this goal. Once you've shared your commitment, you can feel a deeper level of commitment. And now that you've shared it, someone else can feel it, too. Commitment not shared is weak and ineffective. Shared commitment is powerful and effective!

Sharing Accountability

True accountability begins when someone else knows about it – and this leads us to the fourth piece of the Accountability Puzzle: *share*.

When you asked your friend to check in on your progress toward losing 5 pounds, you created an Accountability Partner, a person (or people) who wants to build you up and will invest their time to do so. This partnership is based on the individual or group's intention of assisting you in meeting your goal. This can only be accomplished when you invite them to hold you accountable by checking in and following up with you.

Checking In vs. Following Up

What's the difference between checking in and following up?

Follow-up usually occurs at the end of the project and sounds like this: "Is it done?" or "Can I see your productivity report?" Checking in occurs during the process and sounds like, "I know you're working on project 'X.' How's that going?" or "I know you planned to lose 5 pounds by August 25th. What's your weight today, on August 20th?"

The Value of Accountability Partners

Everyone understands that accountability flows easily downstream. However, in a Culture of Accountability, the law of gravity does not apply. Accountability goes upstream and downstream.

There are many books that stress strength and clarity as major components of leadership – and I agree. However, an often-overlooked component of leadership is vulnerability.

In a Culture of Accountability, "being vulnerable" means that if you want people to proactively share commitments with you, then go first – and whether it's going upstream or downstream – in sharing your commitments with others.

The Accountability Partner is the sustainability insurance if something unforeseen happens. It's a natural human emotion to experience fear when others know what you're responsible for. Yet, to foster higher individual and organizational performance, it's important to overcome that fear and embrace Accountability Partners who will hold you accountable for your commitments. **It is important to invite and welcome people to hold you accountable.**

Holding people accountable downstream is easy. After all, you write their performance reviews. But what about the people upstream? How can you hold them accountable? What if your manager is preventing your project from moving ahead? What if the obstacle is your manager's manager ... or even higher?

Your answer might be, "To hold the upstream accountable would be a career-limiting move." You may be right. But, in a high-accountability culture, it is your responsibility to communicate the truth upstream, and in a way that builds your relationship.

In *Seven Habits of Highly Effective People*, Dr. Stephen Covey introduced the term "relationship capital." His philosophy is that, in working with others, we have the option of either depositing or withdrawing relationship capital. This capital is the goodwill you've created, based on how you behave as well as your personal and professional values. Relationship capital can be found among your co-workers, your managers, your current and prospective clients and anyone else with whom you interact.

As I mentioned earlier, when my assistant reminded me about the preparation I should be doing and I said, "Thank you for reminding me. Thank you for keeping me on track," that was a deposit in my relationship capital with her.

A withdrawal of relationship capital would be to throw down the magazine and snap back, "Don't worry about what I'm doing – I'm your boss ... and I think you have better things to do," and then stomp back to my office.

This scenario is what Covey calls "a pinnacle moment," a teaching opportunity. Regardless of the hat I'm wearing – team member or managing partner – I can use this teaching opportunity to invite our employees and others to hold me to my commitments.

Most people upstream are hungry for the truth. Unfortunately, the higher someone is on the organizational chart, the tougher the truth is to discover.

If you deliver the truth upstream, you have done your job. If you are afraid to deliver the truth upstream, you are not fulfilling your obligation to your team. The challenge is to deliver the truth in a way that is factual – not personal – and includes options to pursue. If you do that in a positive, proactive way, relationships will not be destroyed – they will become stronger.

Imagine the impact if every person in your organization was delivering the truth upstream as well as downstream!

Your Accountability Partners come as a result of you publishing, declaring or announcing your commitments by using pieces of the Accountability Puzzle: Here's my clear expectation, include time specificity and then, the third and fourth pieces, "I'm the owner and I want you to know about it."

Leveraging Relationships

Building relationship capital is ongoing – it never stops. It's something we might not be thinking about when times are good, everyone's making money and everyone is happy. If you're not building it when times are good, however, when times are bad – as I learned during a business failure after 9/11 – you're left emotionally bankrupt.

What I discovered is that some relationships that "appeared" to be healthy were, in fact, simply convenient for the other people. When I needed these people, they were gone.

I could blame them. That would be the easiest and most natural thing to do. However, in a Culture of Accountability and using the mirror/glass measure, I must look in the mirror and see where I could have been better at building those specific relationships in the first place.

On the other hand, if I were looking through the glass, looking for someone to blame, I would have simply said, "Those people weren't being honest" … and my forward movement would have been stymied. I learned that "I must let go to grow" to provide myself an opportunity for better things ahead.

Perhaps enrolling these Accountability Partners more proactively would have made this group more loyal. Perhaps they would have been more willing to work through the tough times with me, as others were. I do not know. What I do know is that building relationships requires time, energy and sharing mutual goals.

It's worth a mention that other relationships had been built in a way that provided me with tremendous support during a difficult time. I'll always be grateful to the people who believed in me and supported me.

Many of our executive clients are CEOs. They report that one reason they accomplish so much through our coaching relationships is because they know I'm going to be following up on the commitments they make. One of the ways I model that dynamic is by announcing with a high level of specificity what commitments I'm making … and then I request that my clients do the same. Knowing they're going to be talking to me becomes a motivation and a reminder for them to keep their commitments.

I, too, experience this dynamic. I coach several executives, so I'm focused on other people's stuff a majority of the time. However, when I work with my own coach, I find myself cramming like a school kid to make sure I execute my commitments before my coach follows up with me.

The mechanism that pushes an organization's execution is the accountability built into relationships. Tough conversations that are uncomfortable are a part of building relationships. There is increased accountability when you ask another person to follow up or check in – to share in this accountability with you.

How do we know if our expectation is clear? Remember S.M.A.R.T.E.R.? Let's review the tool that ensures our expectation is specific, measurable, attainable, results-oriented, trackable, ethical and recorded.

Specific – Have I described and provided a visual of the behaviors and deadlines required for good job performance?

Measurable – Can my request be measured?

Attainable – Is it realistic for this person or this team to achieve and accomplish my request within the stated guidelines?

Results-Oriented – Does this request move us closer to our objective?

Trackable – What milestones will ensure that we are on the right track to accomplish our goals?

Ethical – Is the request legal, moral and ethical?

Recorded – Is there a record or a second person who knows about the request or the effort?

Then, as the project is in progress, track (or check in) to measure progress and follow-up, then measure results.

Here is an example of how it all fits together:

Let's say family schedules have made dinner together during the week virtually impossible. To develop new behaviors, you may make some sort of declaration, like, "I miss seeing all of you at the dinner table. I know schedules are hectic, but I am going to work so we can have a family dinner on Sunday evenings at 6 p.m. It would be great if you would help by scheduling your activities to make sure we're all free to have dinner together at 6 on Sundays."

If your family members agree to this plan, you've created shared accountability in the household. You've made every family member an Accountability Partner in achieving the goal of one family dinner a week on Sundays.

You've also made your request using all four pieces of the Accountability Puzzle: You've made it clear – you want to have a family dinner. You've made it time specific – you want to plan these dinners for 6 p.m. every Sunday. You've taken ownership. By making the request, you've also shared with others and created Accountability Partners.

Sharing Accountability

Years ago, we had a client in an electronics company who complained that people didn't give her feedback and never offered input. But when we observed her leading a meeting, we found she dominated every meeting. She didn't give the others a chance to speak and, in fact, her dominating style made her people unwilling to share their own insights.

When we discussed her style with her, we identified benefits of her speaking last at the meetings. Some of the benefits included collecting the wisdom and insights of the team members without unduly influencing them with her suggestions.

From our discussion, she would begin speaking last in meetings. She declared this intention to us and then asked her direct reports to hold her accountable for her commitment. Upon hearing her intention – and then being asked to hold her accountable – the team members didn't feel they would be shut down if the director started to talk first and somebody reminded her, "Hey, boss! I thought you were going to speak last."

When the boss apologized and said she had forgotten about the new arrangement, they felt encouraged.

This is how shared accountability can make you better. It's a relationship builder. By asking your team to become Accountability Partners, you're making deposits of relationship capital. It's as easy as making a commitment, declaring your intention and then asking others to hold you accountable.

Sometimes it may seem that by asking others to fulfill the role of an Accountability Partner, you may be burdening them with "more work." While it may seem counterintuitive, **most people have a natural tendency to want to help**, particularly if you have helped them first. Asking people to be your Accountability Partner can be a great relationship builder.

Here's something you can begin doing now … today. It's likely you interact with other people as part of your job – and you probably interact with these same people on a regular basis. Why not be a resource to them in their own performance? Make yourself available to be an Accountability Partner as they make their own commitments.

Summary:

1. Accountability begins when two or more people know about a commitment.

2. Accountability goes upstream and downstream.

3. You go first!

4. Relationship capital must be deposited continually.

Your Role in Creating an Accountability Culture

The first great gift we can bestow on others is a good example.
Thomas Morell

In creating a Culture of Accountability within your organization, keep these important steps in mind as you begin your journey:

Step One: Front-Loading Expectations

If you front-load with clear expectations, specific dates and time, clear ownership and a shared understanding, you're going to experience better outcomes.

Step Two: You Have the Power

The power in an organization comes from those leading it … regardless of where they show up on the organizational chart. In high-accountability cultures, the true leader is anyone who reverses the negative momentum of an interaction so that it is focused on a solution.

Step Three: Look Into the Mirror, Not the Glass

Remember the mirror/glass theory? If we look through the glass window, it's easy to see what others are doing wrong, and we invest our mental energy in determining what others should be doing. More constructive feedback comes from looking into the mirror – at ourselves. By evaluating what we're doing that's right, as well as where we could improve, we are able to move ahead in a more positive direction.

Step Four: Model What You Wish to Achieve

I invite you to imagine this for a moment: What if every member of your organization was focused on their personal communication, the quality of their communication and also was willing to improve it?

Can you fathom what would happen to your organization? What if every person in your organization focused on how effectively they themselves were using these accountability principles, as opposed to looking out the window to criticize others?

When every member focuses on the quality of their communication, the organization begins breeding accountability. The organization then magically transforms into a culture where people invite others to hold them accountable, and hold others accountable in a safe and productive manner.

A Clear Expectation
+ Specific Dates and Times
+ An Owner
+ Sharing
_____
Stronger Relationships,
which then create personal
and professional success.

When each member begins practicing personal accountability for his/her commitments, and is willing to take ownership and recruit Accountability Partners, a higher level of performance begins to emerge.

Why does this happen? When we align our thoughts and words with the outcome we desire, we create an "intentional action." **An intentional action occurs when your thoughts, words and actions are in alignment with your desired outcomes and/or goals.**

Is it easy to create a Culture of Accountability? Of course not. Making the changes necessary to establish a Culture of Accountability takes practice, modeling and encouragement. But as more members of your organization begin using the four pieces of the Accountability Puzzle, you'll begin to see more efficiency, more confidence and more productivity as a result.

Historically, Dynamic Results' clients have achieved and completed 86 percent of their strategic plans by using the Accounability Methods discussed in the book. Our clients achieve this level of success because *every* action that is connected to *any* strategic initiative has our Accountability Method attached to it. Each action has a clearly defined expectation with measurement (first piece of the puzzle), a specific date and time for completion (second piece of the puzzle) and one owner per task (third piece of the puzzle). All of these commitments are presented (in person) and then published out to the team to share (fourth piece of the puzzle).

But what about the 90 percent of other organizations that fail to implement strategic plans successfully? They could have saved a lot of time and money by simply going to an office supply store, buying binders, writing "Strategic Plan" on the front and sticking them on the shelf. As one client learned, until they had worked on their Culture of Accountability, almost all of their strategic plans ended up as "shelfware" – because they were developed and then shelved for lack of implementation.

The fact is that implementing a strategy involves a willingness to be imperfect and the courage to proceed without all of the necessary information and to move ahead when things are uncertain.

The First Step Begins with You

Remember in Chapter One when we asked you to write down a couple of commitments? We would like for you to take these same commitments and rewrite them now, using the four pieces of the Accountability Puzzle.

Business Commitment: _____

_____

_____

Personal Commitment: _____

_____

_____

_____

If you're like most people we've worked with in this method, you'll see a sharp change between what you originally wrote and what you've written now. Most people report their original commitments were ambiguous and lacked specificity, compared to the second version. So, if yours improved or changed from the first time you wrote them, you've already taken the first step in building a Culture of Accountability.

It's also important to remember: With the Culture of Accountability, we're not offering a series of measures to punish people in your organization ... measures that would kill relationships. Instead, we're offering tools that will help you set clear objectives and build those necessary key relationships.

You will discover that accountability is positive, productive and relationship-building when you follow the steps outlined in this book!

Summary:

1. Accountability in organizations rests with the individuals who lead it. Remember: The "leader" is anyone on the organizational chart who reverses the momentum of a negative interaction.

2. If accountability is front-loaded with clear expectations, specific dates and time, clear ownership and a shared understanding, you will experience better outcomes.

3. Thoughts drive feelings and feelings drive actions. Always operate from a place where your thoughts and feelings are in alignment with your desired outcomes and/or goals.

NEXT STEPS

Theory without application produces nothing.

We've given you some concepts that are intellectually simple, meaning you can understand them – and you already do, but they are behaviorally complex and require practice.

Here are a few suggestions to get you started.

First, we suggest you go back and review the Four Pieces of the Accountability Puzzle. For updated approaches to increasing accountability in your organization, register for our free newsletter, *The Dynamic Perspective*, by visiting www.WinningWithAccountability.com.

You will also find **Countdown Timers** – an easy-to-use tool to help team members remain aware of promised deadlines, important presentations and meetings. The Countdown Timer is much like

NASA's countdown to shuttle liftoffs, only it sits on your desk and you can program it. On any day and at any time, team members know exactly how much time they have to complete a task or assignment.

This makes the time you have to achieve something *real*. Instead of saying "we have three months" to do this, you look at your countdown timer and say "we have 78 days, 9 hours and 43 minutes to complete this task."

Next, share this book with others and begin practicing these principles. The more people in your organization who can walk the accountability talk, the better your results will become.

Then, practice by:

+ Reviewing your calendar for the past two weeks. Think about the meetings and commitments you've made or requested and see how they compare to the language of specificity found in four pieces of the Accountability Puzzle.

+ Making corrections. Send e-mails or memos, providing any information you think was missing in the original request. It may sound like:

   Dear Erika, As part of my effort to develop both personally and professionally, I'm focusing on making more specific requests and commitments. When I reread the commitment I made to you last week, I felt it was incomplete. I notice I didn't tell you when I would have the third-quarter report to you, and I'm following up now to give you a specific date.

+ Demonstrating your commitment to self-development. You may say, "I thought I was clear in communicating that task to you last week, John. As I think about it now, I don't think I was. I know what I meant to say, but what did you hear?"

Also, practice imbedding the four pieces of the Accountability Puzzle in your requests and commitment. Here's an example: "I (ownership) promise to ship you a poster-sized, full-color accountability puzzle (clear expectation), by Tuesday, August 29, at 5 p.m. EST (specific date and time), and I just wanted you to know it's coming (share)."

Ask people to reflect upon the direction that you have provided. Earlier in my own career, I wasn't good at this. I asked people to repeat back what I had said, verbatim. What I was really after was the essence of what I said … just in their words.

As an example, instead of saying, "Now, tell me what I said, word for word," which insults the intelligence of anyone, demonstrate your vulnerability by saying, "I know what I meant to say just now, but what did you hear?" Or, you could also say, "How did you interpret what I just said?"

If the individual comes back to you with something totally different, it probably will happen again if you don't change your communication style with this particular individual.

Leveraging your Skills to Create a Culture of Accountability

✦ On an accountability level, a Culture of Accountability begins with you. Don't wait for the company to change. Be the change.

✦ Work with an Accountability Partner. Show others you're willing to be accountable for your own commitments by inviting them to check in – and thanking them when they do.

✦ Be vulnerable. Be a model. Keep working on your personal accountability, at work and in your life away from your job.

Accountability is for fearless individuals who are not content with the status quo ... individuals who want to be true agents of change. With accountability, you will be more productive, reaching higher levels of your performance potential. You'll also experience richer interactions and relationships with others, both professionally and personally, and there will be no barriers to what you'll achieve.

True accountability begins in the language you use when making and requesting commitments. You choose your words, so why not choose them carefully, speak intentionally, and influence the kind of change you wish to see by building a strong, high-performing culture? Be a model, "go first," and start using the Language of Accountability today.

Integrity is not in a statement. Integrity is in the actions that follow your statement.

A CHAPTER-BY-CHAPTER QUICK REFERENCE

CHAPTER ONE FRONT-LOADING ACCOUNTABILITY

1. Accountability is a positive term describing commitments that – in the eyes of others – have been kept.

2. Accountability is continually asking, "How am I doing?"

3. To front-load accountability in your organization, you have to provide crystal-clear expectations.

4. By front-loading accountability, relationships among team members are strengthened because they know they can count on each other. This leads to greater performance, higher quality and better service to your clients.

CHAPTER TWO YOU LOOKING AT ME?

1. Building a Culture of Accountability requires time, patience and vision ... and begins with you.

2. People are watching everything you do. You are always leading one direction or another.

3. First, focus on yourself when determining what might have gone wrong.

4. Ask yourself: Did I communicate clear expectations? Did I include the right people in initial discussions? What could I have done better?

5. Create accountability partners ... people you invite to hold you accountable for specific tasks.

CHAPTER THREE The Language of Accountability

1. A Culture of Accountability is a culture where all team members hold each other accountable for their commitments in a positive and productive manner.

2. "Potholes" occur when specificity of language is missing, particularly in making commitments. These potholes can be filled in with specific and accountable information.

3. The Glossary of Failure contains the language we use that forecasts relationship or project failure. It's ambiguous, lacks specificity and will assuredly lead to disappointment, failure and bad feelings.

4. The opposite of the Glossary of Failure is the Language of Accountability … the Language of Specificity.

5. It's the leader's job to reverse the momentum of negative interactions – and anyone can be the leader.

CHAPTER FOUR I Can See Clearly Now

1. The first piece of the Accountability Puzzle is clarity. When we make a request with clear expectations we create a visual representation all parties can see, and the team will be motivated, focused and working on the right thing.

2. If specificity is missing in your request, accountability gaps are created.

3. The first step in bridging these accountability gaps is setting clear, visual expectations, replacing ambiguity with specificity.

4. Do not confuse "accountability" with "consequences." They are related ... and different. Consequences should simply be stated as part of setting clear expectations. By communicating consequences as part of a front-loaded clear expectation, we have created accountability!

CHAPTER FIVE   It's Time to Get Specific

1. The Language of Accountability is specific about dates, times and time zones. It's also realistic when it comes to managing time and aligning priorities with time and resources available.

2. Time specificity, which is vital to creating a Culture of Accountability, works with timelines, not deadlines.

3. Time specificity can protect your integrity.

CHAPTER SIX   Ownership

1. Only one person should be the owner of a task. A team cannot own a task.

2. The buck stops with the owner of a project ... even if every task has been delegated.

3. Assign ownership by competency first, bandwidth (time) second.

4. Today's organizational chart should support your vision of tomorrow's organization.

CHAPTER SEVEN   GOING PUBLIC

1. Accountability begins when two or more people know about a commitment.

2. Accountability goes upstream and downstream.

3. You go first!

4. Relationship capital must be deposited continually.

CHAPTER EIGHT   YOUR ROLE IN CREATING A HIGH-ACCOUNTABILITY CULTURE

1. Accountability in organizations rests with the individuals who lead it.

2. If accountability is front-loaded with a clear expectation, specific dates and time, clear ownership and a shared understanding, you will experience better outcomes.

3. Thoughts drive feelings and feelings drive actions. Always operate from a place where your thoughts and feelings are in alignment with your desired outcomes and/or goals.

ABOUT THE AUTHOR

Henry J. Evans is the co-founder and managing partner of Dynamic Results, an organizational development firm delivering results to organizations around the world.

Henry applies the knowledge and experience gleaned from numerous successes and a failure in his own career, augmented by the knowledge gained in working with his executive clients.

Henry has been interviewed twice by Entrepreneur magazine and, in 2007, he twice earned the Business Leadership Center's Teaching Excellence Award at the SMU Cox School of Business in Dallas where he also is an instructor.

His life mission is to "leave every person and situation better than I found them."

Henry may be reached at hevans@dynamicresults.net

ACKNOWLEDGEMENTS

I'm genuinely influenced by and learn something from everyone I meet. Here are those whom I remembered to mention:

First off, my mother, Norma, for inspiring my creative spirit, and my father, Carl, for modeling what it means to – throughout life – work to improve one's level of understanding and compassion. And to both of my parents for loving me unconditionally.

My grandparents – Louis, Anna, Henry and Pauline – for bravely enduring hardships that no human being should ever have to bear so that my parents and I could have a better life.

Ana Lucia, who is my love, my life, and who diligently helped me formulate my thoughts during final editing. You make me a better man.

David, Bruce and Steve for always believing in me, even when I had trouble believing in myself. Bob and Mike for tangibly helping me when I needed it. Sherna, whom I have never heard say anything negative about another human being. Jennifer, who has, by example, led me "across the rocks" since the age of 3. Jenny, for supporting and challenging me for years. Aela, for unwavering creativity and drive when producing this work. Mike and Chenoa, who took time away from their own careers and beautiful son to help me in the final stages.

The incredible team of experts at Dynamic Results who thrill our clients … and challenge me to be a better man and leader.

My good friends on the advisory board – Wendy and Adam – for always inspiring both clear and creative thought.

David Cottrell, my publisher, for calmly and strongly leading and mentoring me through the process of producing my book. Your faith and wisdom helped bring this book to fruition. To my production team, Alice, Kathleen, Melissa and Nick, who always find a way to bring my muddy ideas into clear, graphical form.

My Aunt Jackie and Uncle Maurice, who took me out of NYC every summer to show me mountains and oceans.

Also, to mentors whom I may have or have not met: Mahatma Gandhi, Dr. Martin Luther King Jr., T.E. Lawrence, "John," the Dalai Lama, Muhammed Ali, Tony, Jimmy, "Bobby the boss," Eddie Rivera (who was my first model on how to have crucial conversations), and Greg Jackson (the embodiment of a good leader).

Finally, my clients. This group of individuals challenges me to be better, shape our work, and inspire me to be as great as they are. They have the courage to face real issues, both individual and organizational, and work through them. I am honored to receive their trust.

Because of our commitment to confidentiality, I won't mention them by name, but let me say that if you live in an industrialized nation, you are likely to prepare your food, use energy, exercise, drive safely, live in well-managed housing, and enjoy public safety (and security) as a result of our intelligent, thoughtful, caring, capable, and dedicated clients.

Due to my own oversight, I've probably neglected to mention some people who are very important to me. I trust they will accept my apology and know that, with or without mention here, I value them greatly.

More Ways to Create
High-Accountability Cultures
with Your Team

1. Keynote Presentations and Workshops

Invite author Henry J. Evans – or one of our certified facilitators – to help your team accelerate their journey to higher performance. Our practical approach to creating, energizing and engaging presentations will create instant take-away value for your team. Material includes additional aspects of our accountability method not covered in the book. For more information, visit **www.dynamicresults.net** or contact us at 214-742-1403, x102.

2. The Accountability Puzzle Laminated Wallet Cards

These laminated wallet cards are kept in the pockets of executives all over the world for easy reference. With this full-color depiction of the Accountability Puzzle, executives can stick them to their computer monitors or phones for reminders of what to say (and listen for) in order to have truly accountable dialogues. Fast, easy visual reference for success!
Pk/10 (3" x 2") $49.95   www.CornerStoneLeadership.com

3. The Accountability Puzzle Wall Poster

Hold each other accountable in meeting environments with these full-color depictions of the Accountability Puzzle. Hanging in executive offices, boardrooms and conference rooms all over the world, these posters will help your team hold productive meetings that produce results! Refer to this poster and get rid of "wiggle room" when commitments are being made during meetings.
Framed (18" x 24"), $89.95. Poster print only, $19.95
www.CornerStoneLeadership.com

4. Achieve with Excellence Countdown Timer

This electronic countdown timer sits on your desk and counts down the days, hours, minutes and seconds to your programmable deadline. Attractive graphics remind you to "Achieve with Excellence" while you focus on "Next Steps." Artwork depicts mountain climbers making their way to a peak. **$29.95 each www.CornerStoneLeadership.com**

5. *Winning with Accountability* Assessment

Take this free, online assessment based on the *Winning with Accountability* book. A five-minute investment yields a quick perspective on how your organization stacks up against truly accountable cultures! Complimentary.

Visit **www.dynamicresults.net**

Recommended Reading

Monday Morning Mentoring is an expanded and enhanced hardcover version of best-selling *Monday Morning Leadership*. It includes new sessions on how to deal with change and constructive feedback. Hardcover **$19.95**

7 Moments … That Define Excellent Leaders
The difference between average and excellent can be found in moments … literally. These moments shape the leaders we are and the leaders we will become. Seize the moment to read and apply, and you will be one step closer to leadership excellence! **$14.95**

The Eight Constants of Change is a practical, easy-to-use guide that can help you and your team generate immediate, tangible and positive results. While change is not easy, this straightforward and entertaining book offers your management team a framework for working through the challenges of change. Employing *The Eight Constants of Change* process will buoy employee morale and improve your bottom line … beginning immediately. **$14.95**

The Manager's Conflict Resolution Handbook should be required reading for every manager on your team! The strategies in this book work! They provide a structure for handling conflict and information about what to do when the unexpected happens. **$14.95**

Leadership Energy (E=mc²) provides a step-by-step strategy to access your organization's energy reservoir and, through the use of this energy, accelerate your organization to the next level. As you read, you'll discover Synchronization, Speed, Communication, Customer Focus, and Integrity − five vital energy conductors to help you energize your team, customers and profits. **$14.95**

The Nature of Excellence **Gift Book** − Stunning photography and inspirational quotes are combined in *The Nature of Excellence* 88-page, coffee-table-size book. Through the twin lens of insight and imagery, you'll discover the natural excellence that surrounds us. You will also learn from the wisdom of more than 100 successful people who have inspired excellence throughout history. Hardcover **$29.95**

YES! Please send me extra copies of *Winning with Accountability!*
1-30 copies $14.95   31-100 copies $13.95   101+ copies $12.95

Winning with Accountability _____ copies X _____ = $ _____

Recommended Reading

Monday Morning Mentoring _____ copies X _____ = $ _____

7 Moments That Define Excellent Leaders _____ copies X _____ = $ _____

The Eight Constants of Change _____ copies X _____ = $ _____

Leadership Energy _____ copies X _____ = $ _____

The Manager's Conflict Resolution Handbook _____ copies X _____ = $ _____

The Nature of Excellence Gift Book _____ copies X _____ = $ _____

Shipping & Handling $ _____

Subtotal $ _____

Sales Tax (8.25%-TX Only) $ _____

Total (U.S. Dollars Only) $ _____

Shipping and Handling Charges

Total $ Amount	Up to $49	$50-$99	$100-$249	$250-$1199	$1200-$2999	$3000+
Charge	$7	$9	$16	$30	$80	$125

Name _____ Job Title_____

Organization _____ Phone_____

Shipping Address _____ Fax _____

Billing Address_____ E-mail _____
(required when ordering PowerPoint® Presentation)

City_____ State _____ ZIP_____

❑ Please invoice (Orders over $200) Purchase Order Number (if applicable)_____

Charge Your Order: ❑ MasterCard   ❑ Visa   ❑ American Express

Credit Card Number _____ Exp. Date_____

Signature _____

❑ Check Enclosed (Payable to: CornerStone Leadership)

Fax	**Mail**	**Phone**
972.274.2884	P.O. Box 764087	888.789.5323
	Dallas, TX 75376	

www.**CornerStoneLeadership**.com

Thank you for reading *Winning with Accountability*.
We hope it has assisted you in your quest for
personal and professional growth.

CornerStone Leadership is committed to providing new
and enlightening products to organizations worldwide.
Our mission is to fuel knowledge with practical resources
that will accelerate your team's productivity,
success and job satisfaction!

Best wishes for your continued success.

CornerStone
Leadership Institute
www.CornerStoneLeadership.com

*Start a crusade in your organization –
have the courage to learn, the vision to lead,
and the passion to share.*